POETRY FOR THE SOUL

VOLUME I

BY

MADAME BUTTERFLI

madamebutterfli.com
PO Box 34093
St. Louis, MO 63134
www.madamebutterfli.com
Cover photo: Eric Pierre
Interior Design: Manika Felix

Poetry for the Soul: Heavenly Inspiration/ Madame Butterfli. -- 2nd edition 2015

ISBN-13: 978-0615970226
ISBN-10: 0615970222

DEDICATION

To my one and only true, living God

To my two angels Valeri Candyce and Alano Zecharias. You inspire me every day to keep pushing, praying, and dreaming

I love you.

Prologue

I give thanks unto the Lord, who is truly worthy of all praise

Those who praise his name will be raised

So much you have done for me known and unknown, seen and unseen

The Lord is good, he holds his children at the highest esteem

He is our father, gift bearer, our protector, the great physician, and lily of the valley

Our every burden he carries

So I give him thanks for what he has already done

I praise him in advance for every battle that is about to be won

A Better Me

Like a tree planted by the water, I shall not be

moved

Like water flowing down the river, I will have

peace

Like the sun shining high in the sky, I will be a light

to the world

Like an eagle flying above the clouds, I will watch

for your soul

I will be, a better me

A Place Called Peace

There is a place called peace where love abides

There is a place called peace that evilness cannot
find

There is a place called peace, in it my soul rests

It gives me advantage during trials and tests

There is a place called peace that floats like a cloud

that brings laughter to my spirit and wipes away my
frown

There is a place called peace where joy is king

There is no frustration, only freedom and happiness
in every situation

Where is this place? It's in your heart and mind

Seek and you will find it every time

A Way Out

You may be weeping now, but joy comes in the morning

Let anyone who rises against you have fair warning

Our God of love will fill your cup,

he sees every tear and bottles them up

Trust your battle and time of struggle

God will reward you and give you double

Keep on trusting, never doubt

It will be soon that he reveals your way out

All That I Have

I surrender all that I have to you

Your faithfulness is above all

It's because of you that I rise

I humble my heart, there is no disguise

All that I have is yours, use me as you please

to break down walls and free others from captivity

According to your will, I walk

With your words, I will talk

I surrender all that I have unto you

Lead me in your direction,

while keeping me safe with angels of protection

Anew

Corruption cannot dwell in the majestic company of the most high

Those who will not conform will be cast down

His goodness must overflow from your heart, captivate your thoughts

Your lives shall be increased instead of decreased

You are made whole and anew

Your life is based in tranquility

Excellent words shall proceed from your lips

Your feet will not run to mischief

You take pleasure in doing what is good in God's sight

My God is a gentleman, he does not force his way upon any

Blessed are those who willingly walk in his
principles

They shall reap his rewards all the days of their
lives

Apologies

Never underestimate the power of an apology

Even though you may not agree, two words can
keep you from your destiny

A repentant heart is one that is sober

not drunken with pride, arrogance, or deceit

It puts you on a higher ground and away from
defeat

Humility apologizes when others may be at fault

A healthy heart is a clean heart

It has a mind that is free and full of gratitude,

joyous, and happy, with a positive attitude

As a Child

As a child, I seek your approval desperate to come into your gates

Like a child without a father, longing for an embrace

I want to be just like you, model you in every way

Teach me all things, hold my hand so that I don't go astray

Unlike a natural father, you will be with me forever

I'll look up to you and worship you through all types of weather

As a child, I look to your face

to see you smile at my work as I go to a higher place

Be Free

The power of God will free all that are bound

Prisoners to opinions, fear, compromise for gain,

addictions, depression, abuse, and pain

Turn it over to him, allow God to renew, revive, and heal

He is able to break the chains, set free the captives

Remove every curse, turn mourning to laughter

You must obey and follow his lead,

no longer seek to be bound, but to rise up and proceed

Walking towards the greatness that he has for you in life

Leaving behind all of the anger, bitterness, and strife

going to a place where freedom resides

Free and clear from the chains in your mind

Be Right

You never know who the person next to you may be

An angel unaware or sent by the enemy

Be kind to others, watch, and pray

Be careful to lead them in the right way

Have the integrity to do what is right no matter
who's around

It will lead you to higher grounds

You never know what a person needs

Be gentle, caring, and do good deeds

Every day we live our purpose with actions big and
small

They add up to greatness and become worship, most
important of all

Calls to Heaven

Calls to heaven never cost a thing

Anytime, anyplace, just ask the Lord to intervene

He hears you when you cry out with and humble
heart

Prayer is the glue that keeps life from falling apart

Prayers of thanksgiving or of suffering and need,

your call to heaven will be answered on the first
ring

Prayer brings forgiveness, restoration, and peace

Whether you are crying loud or whispering

you will be heard, God knows your voice

He will intervene at any cost

Christmas

Would I sacrifice my son to be scorned?

Send him to the earth by a virgin to be born?

Take him from paradise to earth,

From being worshiped by angels, to being cursed?

Yet God loved us so, he sent a savior

To save us from the consequences of our unruly
behavior

I am grateful this day for the birth of Christ

Who came so that we may have eternal life

Covered

Praises will flow like a fountain from my belly

My God is deserving of them all

He fills my heart with radiance and laughter

He keeps my mind in perfect peace

I wake up each day to honor him, beyond grateful
that he delivered me from myself

The full knowledge of his might is true wealth

I run after my savior, the redeemer of the lost

Because of him, we bear no cost

He has covered it all

Covered With His Mercy

He showers me with his kindness, covers me with
his mercy

There is privilege in knowing my God, treasure in
his occupancy

Because all that is good comes from him,

I do not hesitate to follow him out on a limb

For in my solid rock, there is divine protection

I shall not fear, but be confident

My being is not coincidental

Though nothing is simple, I will still trust and stand

Knowing that my God has the power of the world in
his hands and, in spite of it all, I am yet showered
with his kindness

Covered by his mercy

Daylight

The darkness of night is only temporary

As the sun rises, so does a new dawn

Blessed for the previous, but happy that it's gone

Embrace what is before you, never stop seeking

Take advantage of every moment to keep your

territory from shrinking

We were created as an image of God to rule this

land

Yet, we give our power over into the enemy's hands

Take charge over what you have been given,

because just as the night, your daylight is limited

Dear God

You keep me through the hardest times

Your faithfulness I can't deny

No matter how the situation may seem

I remember that you are God of everything

You turned a sea into dry land

The power of the world is in your hands

I do not fear what comes against me

One thousand on my left, ten thousand on my right

With "mustard seed" faith, they will all flee

When tears are falling and I feel so weak

You pick me up and carry me if I fall at your feet

Divine Eyes

No one really knows what is in store

Our limited vision can only see what is right before

If we look to the master and creator of all

he will further our grasp,

enlarge our territory, if we ask

Renew your mind daily, surrender completely

Only what we do for Christ will last

You will go the furthest when you place your all
into God's hands

His vision is broader than the skies

He created you in his image, so ask for his divine
eyes

He knows what is best and already has a plan in

mind-

guaranteed to be better than yours

Trust him, it's just a matter of time

Divine Healing

No need for despair, the virtue of God fills the air

The healer of every sickness and disease

The remedy is prayer, don't neglect to fall down on
your knees

He will touch your body among many other things

The side effects of prayer are positive in reaction

You will receive much more than you were asking

God will take control of every aspect, he created
man from the dust

He is the master surgeon that I trust for healing
divine

No need for despair, my God is right there

His virtue fills the air

Don't be Afraid

There is no need to be afraid

Our dear father even has power over the grave

Look to heaven for what can't be explained,

praying and relenting to his holy name

We can do nothing with our own might,

totally surrender and follow his light

Our own ways will take us farther away

within his realm, it is best to stay

Our own minds will take us to dark places, they are
fragile and weak

no matter how strong you think you may be

We will compete because we are afraid

while at the cross our burdens should have been laid

Fully rely on God, there is rest in him

He will brighten a path that was once dim

Dreams

Our dreams are created by what is inside

What drives us gives us the ability to thrive

We are created to do what is in our heart

God takes over when we do our part

Your best will go above and beyond what you have
ever thought

Just take courage and begin to walk

towards the place that you have already been shown

Reap the harvest that has been sown

Your dreams are not a coincidence, they are created
by what you have inside

Your real value and purpose can no longer hide

Endless Mercy

The mercy of God is endless

He has special care for the defenseless

Keep your eyes on him

Fight until you win

His favor gives you strength to endure to the end

Put your faith in the most trusted friend

He'll give you wings like an eagle to soar

above life's trials, famine, and war

Endless mercy is given to us, if in God we trust

He sets us free from captivity

allows us to thrive until we meet him in eternity

Eternally Bound

Though I've seen rough days and wondered why

there is always a lesson, a moral, I learn something
to live by

God is the shade upon my right hand, I will never
leave his side

My life begins and ends with Jehovah, there is no
way to deny

All else is temporal: people, places, and things

knowing this, allegiance my heart will sing

Master, Savior, Lover, and King

Provider, Healer, Protector, amongst other things

I could go on for days praising his name

Having full knowledge that within myself, I was
walking towards an early grave

But God kept his hand upon me

For that, I am eternally bound to the King

Excellent

God is excellent in thought and deed

He is the standard that I will work to achieve

To be like Christ, made in his image and mine

able to stand the test of time

dependable, true, never forsaking me or you

lover of our soul, creating new from old

Strong tower, friend, supplier of needs til no end;

encourager, protector, uplifter, healer, motivator

The list goes on about our saviour

He is the standard by which we should live;

of ourselves constantly give

Excellent in thought and deed

accomplished by acknowledging his word and

taking heed

To be like Christ is simpler than it seems

Surrender your life and watch him do amazing
things

Faith

My trust in you takes me to new heights

Through my burdens, I continue to fight

I have already won,

new life has begun

I am delighted by your word

my every prayer is heard

My faith in you just continues to grow

With you I know, that I am never alone

Faithful and True

There is one who is faithful and true,

who does all that is required for him to do

He cares for his people in every way-

hand feeding his word, just as scattering seed for
birds

A servant, protector, defender, and friend

creator and lover beginning to end

Faithful and true, you can always count on him

Every morning anew he will be there for you

Father

In your loving arms I rest,

such peace and stillness there

Wrapped within your wings of love is the best

You take care of me, just as the fowl of the air

Father I call you, savior and friend

My heart is grateful, my life complete

You satisfy my soul to no end

Fill Me Up

Fill my cup, use me up

I won't be satisfied until there is nothing left in
storage

I submit my life to God, the author of my story;

to be a character with character is the desire of my
heart

My life is in the most precious hands,

the director who tells me when to stop and start

Continue to cleanse my heart, make me fit for the
best

With you alone I will pass every test,

to go where you will have me and say what is
required,

to be a true servant, not just one for hire

I am yielded with my hands lifted high

As I offer praises to you, your spirit is nigh

Take over, guide me, and fill my cup

All that I have is yours, use me up

For Christ

Only you can make your promises come to pass

I know that what I do for Christ will last

My selfish ambitions are all in vain

I have no issue with yielding to your name

I no longer seek to think my own thoughts

Yours are far greater than whatever I was taught

Your way is much easier than I could have
imagined

You renew me every step of the way, my heart is
not abandoned

I try, but I fail when I do it my way

Only you can make your promises come to pass

All things that I do for Christ will last

Forward

Tranquility of spirit, wholeness of mind

Leave all of your worries and doubts behind

Walk forward to what is ahead,

towards the mark being Spirit led

Fear starved, faith fed

"You can do all things," is what He said

Though you may be weary and misunderstood

Believe, endure, you will be steadfast and secure

Know that all will work together for good

Keep pressing, don't stop,

moving forward

Free

My spirit has wings to fly

above all anger, hurt, and despair

As I dwell on what is good, my thoughts lift me into
the air

above the birds that sing and the clouds that loom

Away from darkness and gloom

into a place that is wonderfully made, designed just
for me

full of comfort and contentment, no one with strife
or resentment

Only those who harbor peace, who laugh in the face
of defeat

whose spirits also fly

We'll join together in a chorus saying, "Above all, I
rise!"

Freedom

There is such freedom in the presence of the Lord

Heavy hearts are lifted, chains are broken

Freedom from bondage in every area that the word
of God is spoken

There is liberty where the spirit of the Lord lives

Confidence and love it gives

Seek it, ask for it

you shall receive it and live in Jesus' name

Friend of God

Blessed is the one who is a friend of God,

who leans to the Son when times get hard

Never disappointed, always fulfilled

All is well with his soul, new life revealed

Clouds arise and storms pass through

In safety he dwells, no matter what weather is due

His sources are plentiful, health and marrow fill his
bones

Sounds of gladness are within his soul, rejoicing
daily while he grows old

The advantage of being a friend of God, all that
know him are shown

If the world turns against me, who do I call?

Jesus, true friend of us all

You know all about us, yet your love never changed

We can rely on your passion to remain

A true friend, who has never breathed a lie

I bow to you and you lift me high

Fullness

Your love embraces me, captures me, enslaves me

Exquisite like a Rose of Sharon, never leaves my
soul barren

Your Spirit gives me composure, life due to
exposure

Your touch awakens and revives

You are never late, but right on time

I never run empty, your love keeps on filling me,

making it possible to do the impossible

Keeping me fully engaged, only fleeting thoughts of
another

You are worth all of my attention

As long as you speak I will listen to your melodic
voice

I need no other choice

You are my menu, may this love continue

I will dwell in the fullness of your power

My strength increases as I lean on you every second
of the hour

Your grace is sufficient for me, washing away all
darkness

With your guiding light, I see all that you sacrificed
to make provision

The path no longer covered or hidden

Permitting me to follow and dwell in the fullness of
our power

Grateful for the blessings that you have bestowed
upon me,

your flower

Give Thanks

I thank you Lord for the blood you shed with so
much love

Your mercy that abounds when trials attempt to take
us down

You've paid the price for our freedom and joy

Give selflessly, even when we live carelessly

I thank you for not giving up on us

Even when we don't seek you and give you all of
our trust

Because of you, I'm thankful every day, for guiding
my path and leading the way

I honor you and give praise where it is due, and you
continue to bless me through and through

Giver of Peace

Giver of peace, your words are delectable

They make me want to hear more of your excellence,

casting out fear and despair

bringing hope and life, my heart you repair

Preparing me to tell the world all that I hear

passing on knowledge so clear

Devotion from my heart I give,

speaking life to those who will to live

Your secrets in plain sight, but hidden

Just ask and be forgiven

The giver of peace will reconcile your soul

and keep you now and as you grow old

God's Children

We are all God's children, made in his image

Every color, shade, and creed

we all came from one seed

Be kind, gracious, and respectful to each other

It's an ungodly thing to kill or slander your brother

It is God's will that we love one another

We are all God's children, created to be free

to praise, to serve, not to be held in captivity

When you look at your neighbor, you should see
your reflection

another being made in God's image of perfection

God's Forgiveness

He who has done no wrong in his eyes, has nothing
to be thankful for

He who has done much wrong is full of thanks

God, you are the giver of redemption,

the source of grace

Your presence is like an out of body experience,

a calm and blissful place

Those who have been there, cannot compare

Those who have never been there, cannot
comprehend

There is no replacement, no fair value

to your love and forgiveness, there is no end

He who walks away from sin, never to return again

treasures being in the thick of your Holy Spirit and
feeling the power therein

God's Love

God's love is like the rain, so pure and sweet

It washes away condemnation, guilt, and defeat

His love causes you to grow tall and strong like the grass

You'll never have to wonder how long it will last

Like rain, it cleanses the air and causes flowers to bloom

Allow the freshness of his love to enter your room

God's love is as wide as the ocean deep

God's love for you is taller that the eldest tree

His love lasts longer than infinity

God's grace is sufficient, it multiplies as we speak

He longs to have you by his side

Take his hand and allow your soul to thrive

Going Up

Keep going up, never looking back

What's best is before you, faith will keep you on
track

Experience is our teacher, never forget

what lies ahead is a greater fit

You've come too far to give up now

Build your trust, remember that it's not luck

Your story has already been written

let it play out

Don't create an alternate ending due to doubt

Good and Perfect

Jesus I give honor to you

The one who died for my sins

who keeps me grounded against the wind

I stand rooted in your word

None of my prayers have gone unheard

Jesus, you lift my soul to higher ground

No greater love can be found

All of my certainty belongs to you

You've brought me through the fire, tried and true

When it's all over, I'll continue to proclaim

Everything good and perfect comes in your name

Grace

The amazing grace of God keeps me, forgives me

Thank you for your Son who shed is blood for me,
cleansed me, renewed me

My heart belongs to you, no greater gift could I
have received

Your grace covers me like a blanket, keeps my
mind from being deceived

What can separate us, not the smallest or biggest
thing

I come to you with my issues and walk away clean

Gratitude

I am grateful that the Lord delivered me from all of
my fears

While I was in mourning, he dried my tears

To trust in God is to have peace of mind

Whatever I need is always right on time

He cleared my mind, replacing my old thoughts
with his

renewing my spirit and restoring my years

To God I am forever grateful, no man can stop my
praise

through him I will live for the rest of my days

If you never answer another prayer, you are still
sufficient

If I never receive the desires of my heart, from your
face I won't depart

You have proven your grace and love towards me

You have blessed me more than the eyes can see

There are no words to express the gratitude in my
mind

Lord, I thank you for being so kind

He Forever Reigns

I will boast of your excellence and favor

Your word will not return void, you are like a sweet
savor

I will continue to strive for your perfection, you
cannot tell a lie

Your love never changes, I am the apple of your eye

My God is swift to hear and slow to speak

he comforts and heals from my infirmities

His aspiration is to keep me for eternity

My heart pours out much joy when I think of his
name,

let heaven and earth proclaim

Let's boast of the excellence and favor of God,

he forever reigns

He Loves Us

Our father loves us in spite of who we are

He does not judge our well appearance, or even our scars

Man looks outwards, God looks at the condition of our heart

He sees our flaws, but knows our potential

His plans for us, exponential

Strive to do what is right, what is perfect in his sight

Don't fall short or take the bait

The reward for walking uprightly is greater

Our father loves us in spite of who we are

Just trust him, he has carried you thus far

He Never Fails

Lover of our soul, all that seek you will find

Let our thoughts soar and our countenance be lifted

You are the giver of all that is good and perfect

let all else be cast away

My existence, my freedom, my fate is only flawless

looking through the glass tinted with you divine

favor

I will rest in your promises, rely on your guidance

chase after your goodness

You never fail

His Will

There is nothing like the will of God, relying on his guidance will bring you no harm

Ask for his instruction, he will cover you on your way,

from every harm and danger until the storm passes away

As the sun rises, new challenges come along

As you understand the word of God, you will be made strong

Your enemy becomes your footstool and will lift you up high

Everyone speaking against you, their land soon to become dry

You can always trust the will of God, there is nothing to fear

If you go down his path, assuredly he will be near

His Voice

When I arise I hear your voice

It flutters in my spirit, it carries me through the
storm

Your voice is an harmonious triplet, that
encourages, leads, and warns

It mentors me for what's ahead, protects me from
present harm

Your voice fills my mind with your will

with what is good and lovely, my spirit heals

I am indebted to your kindness

For it was you that delivered me from spiritual
blindness

leading me on the straight path to wondrous life

In you, Jesus Christ

How, Who, What?

That which is placed inside is greater that I

I will not focus on the why, but search for how

Be who I am created to be

Say and do what I am compelled to

Never worrying about when my reward will come,

knowing that it will be in due time

Confident that where God is taking me will blow

my mind

I Can Do All Things

Encompassed with your love,

I share your promises from above

You could have chosen someone else, but

you chose me in spite of my infirmities

I offer my sacrifice of praise and become better in
every way

Thank you for your healing, your mercy and
guidance

you love me enough to stay by my side and

push me, carry me, over the hills into my destiny

And now, I can do all things through Christ who
strengthens me

I Love You

I love you like I love the sea

calming, serene, and tranquil to me

I love you like my favorite song

your lyrics make me linger on

I love you like a warm cozy night

With you in my life, all of my dreams are in sight

Never depart, stay inside of me

Your presence is essential, your love unconditional

Many don't understand the power of your hands

Without it, I'm so helpless

I take pride in knowing that your love is infinite,

exquisite

the thought of it makes me windless

If it wasn't free, I would be penniless

You're such a gentleman, you've already paid the

cost

That's why I love you

Incomparable

I'll stop looking because there is none left

I've found the one who has power over life and
death

He fills the room, breaks down walls

Every ill condition, he heals them all

His power is incomparable, his spirit comes down
like a heavy weight

It consumes those who are willing to be a vessel

His Holy Spirit is a gift, a prize, a weapon

I am open to receive, what may defile, I allow to
leave

Just to be like him, the one I've found, who is like
no other

Incomparable in power, yet gentle as a flower

I Rest

Thank you for being on whom I can depend

When times get tough and my patience is thin

I have a solid rock that never changes

If I'm in doubt, you fill my pages

I will create joyful noise for you forever

Knowing that things will get better

You are a faithful friend

Always there thick and thin

Rock of ages, your love never changes

I rest in knowing that I can depend on you

No matter what I am going through

You are the cause of my victory

There is none like you

I cast all of my cares

You are a strong tower that breaks every snare

I rest knowing that on you I can

I Run After You

I run after you

Nothing compares to your peace

I run after you

My strength, my redeemer

The healer of my soul

I run after you

To fill my heart with hope, joy, and laughter

You are the source of my gladness

I run after you and I always find you

Bless your holy name

I Strive

I strive,

To never be the woman that's not worthy of trust

To be honest at all costs

To be humble

To be the one that cares even if no one else does

To be a mentor

To be the same under all circumstances

To see the God in others

To take every experience as a lesson

To learn something new everyday

To be at peace

To be positive when surrounded by negativity

To lift people up, not trip them up

To be still and let God fight all of battles

To rest all of my burdens on him, for his purpose
and for my own sanity

To teach all that I know to my children so that they
can be better people, a mother of excellence

I Surrender All

I give my life completely to you

God, I know that you are willing to renew

For all of my past mistakes, you have paid the price

My heart is open, lead me with your divine advice

Navigate me to the straight and narrow

I trust you to care for me just as a sparrow

My eyes will see your glory and everlasting delight

When I walk towards your beacon light

In God We Trust

In God I trust, in God I live

To all else I die

Of myself I freely give

I have no thought for tomorrow

For it has its own sorrow

I give and live in what is before me

Love, strength, provision, and peace

The key to success is not in your possessions or address

It is in knowing The Source

To Him, leave the rest

You are made to be free from distress

Give honor and praise and watch your stature be upraised

In God I trust, in God I live

Of myself, I'll freely give

Just Know

You will never have problems that you can't bear

There's always an answer to your prayer

When times get rough, don't throw in the towel

Just put "the man" on speed dial

When no one else is on the road

He's always willing to carry the load

He sees all, knows all

He's the one that will catch you if you fall

Don't be afraid, don't lose heart

Worry is a trap that keeps you from traveling far

No situation can ever contend

With our one and only TRUE AND LIVING

FRIEND

Just You

When we come into the world, we come alone

There are people here to greet us

When we leave this world, we leave alone

There are people here to see us away

In between, we must choose our destiny

Whether to win or to lose

Our direction is our decision

We have friends and family along the way

They either help us or lead us astray

If you are going the wrong way, change your ticket

Change your destiny

He compels us alone, we comply alone, we
ultimately answer to Him alone

In between, we make daily choices

Within our companions, we distinguish good and
evil voices

To whom will you listen?

In the end, it's just you

Your best bet, is to do what you were called to

Keep Dreaming

I never want to lose the ability to dream,

to move beyond what everything seems

If my mind can take me there, I can accomplish it

I will tap into my source of strength and keep
pushing

I am stronger than any obstacle that I face

I won't stop until I reach the next place

After that, I'll still keep going, aim higher, and push
harder

A dream is only the first step

What you do with the dream, separates you from the
rest

Keep Going

The race is given to those who endure to the end

Don't give up or stop, you are destined to win

Whether it is hot or cold, rain or snow

With every step that you take, you are bound to grow

May your spirit enlarge as you keep your pace, down the straight and narrow due to God's grace

Your win is vital, every step put in place

Your life is a victory, stay steadfast and make history

Be a vessel for movement and change, let the Holy Spirit reign

Liberty

Liberty sings a glorious melody

My heart flutters to the rhythm

My wings dance to the chorus

The children play to the symphony of strings

The sound of liberty changes many things

No more bloodshed in the streets

Our lips will only speak the most beautiful speech

Love will reign, poverty will cease

When liberty fills the air and begins to sing

Life, Liberty, and the Pursuit of Happiness

Where is life?

Where is my liberty?

Who can help me on my pursuit of happiness?

They say that laughter is medicine

Who quenches fires of doubt in my mind,

closes the mouth of defeat?

They say that a broken spirit dries the bones

To pursue happiness is entering a battlefield

What weapon shall I use?

Light

What will you do when the light shines?

Stand and be radiant or conceal and hide?

All secrets will be revealed

Rewards for integrity and maliciousness to be healed

Don't be ashamed of the marks on your sleeve

If you continue to hide them, how can you become clean?

If you ran away, return to the Father, he will not spite

He has compassion for your soul and will cleanse you with his blood and light

So when the light shines you can stand tall and excel,

For demons run to darkness and their special place in hell

Like You

God, your knowledge is above all

Impart within me your wisdom

Guide my thoughts, order my steps

Embody me with your anointing and your presence

I desire to be in your image completely

Grant me the ability to see what you see, hear what
you hear, feel what you feel

My existence on this earth is temporal, but you are
eternal

I am determined to dwell with you hereafter

May my life be pleasing to you

May I be worthy of your everlasting essence

Keep me near to thee

Lily of the Valley

Make me to be like a lily of the valley

Let my presence be like a sweet aroma to your people

Let me be one who stands tall, yet my head hangs low with humility

Clothe me with the beauty of your purity

Allow me to produce an abundance of flowers who are just like you

Let your Holy Spirit flow through me like a medicine, that others may be healed

Allow me to be like Christ, the lily of the valley

Listen

Let us give an ear to what the Lord is saying

Take time to listen while you are praying

There's no need to bombard with many words and
every thought in your mind

He knows them anyway, what's the point of lying?

Always be slow to speak and swift to hear

The goodness of the Lord is guaranteed to appear

Give an ear to what the Lord has to say

It will allow wisdom to follow you all of your days

Made in His Image

I am made in his image

Created divinely from start to finish

Crown with his glory, he wrote my story

Every trial and test prepared me for his best

Child of the King, he makes me ruler over many
things

My desire is to please the one who breathed into
me,

who gave me life abundantly

Now I can sing

My praises move mountains

My eyes see the unseen

My hands tear down wickedness, yet my feet walk
in peace

Made in his image, I am above and not beneath

To me, everything splendid is bequeathed

I am created with destiny and intention for divine

intervention

My Earthly King

You are more valuable that rare pearls, more
beautiful than the clear ocean deep

Add more peace to my heart than a symphony of
strings

I cannot express the bliss that you bring

I never want to hurt you or say the wrong things

I'm loyal to you, my earthly king

Your meaning is endless, you give more happiness
than the world ever could

I love you so much for speaking to my heart

never willing to let enemies tear us apart

Devoted to the avenue of peace

Your crown awaits, my earthly king

My Father's Kingdom

Which way will get me to the father?

I'll be fine once I'm in his kingdom

There are so many paths to take

banners waving for my attention to break

I put my head down to concentrate on my feet and
my direction

All the while, praying for God's guidance and
protection

Keep my intentions pure and my eyes focused,
my mind filled with serenity

While reaching the place that I need to be

The dwelling place of my father, his kingdom

My Friend

To the true and faithful friend,

who is there from beginning to end

Thank you for all that you give

You are my reason to live

Wonderful gifts you have supplied

With them in mind, I continue to thrive

taking no thought for what tomorrow will bring

Grateful for all things

Big or small, nothing taken for granted

I am left in awe, my heart enchanted

by you grace and adequacy, you allow me to be

free and cheerful, never fearful

Blessed abundantly

My God

The greatest gift in the world, is the beauty of your face

My soul longs for your embrace

I am lost without you

You make all of my dreams come true

You stay near to me, loving me completely

never forsaking the creation of your hands

protecting me from the chaos of this land

Replacing all that is lost

I am willing to pay the cost of never leaving your side

I know that it is well worth it,

for nothing compares to the price that you have paid for my liberty

My Greatest Love of All

My greatest love of all is my love for you

When I surrender my heart and mind, you carry me through

You are love, the very context and meaning

allowing your light to gleam through me

You are the source of my being

I surrender to your love, no other is quite the same

For your love is power, bless your holy name

My Trust

My hope and reliance is in the Lord, who knows the
intimate secrets of my heart

I confide in Him daily, pain and confusion he
thwarts

He keeps my mind in perfect peace, he keeps me
rooted as a strong tree

My total reliance is on the Lord, who speaks life to
me continually,

pushing me through the haze into everything that is
in store

I weep no more

He has placed his hand firmly on my shoulders,
whispering in my ear

My Heart

My heart is soft and tender towards you

It cries out with cheer, because my redeemer is near

My cup overflows with praise and sacrifice to your
name

Grace unmerited you give to us, favor and power

I desire to worship you every hour

Inhabit me daily

Take control of this vessel, order my life

Empty it of all anger and strife

Circumcise my heart, keep it soft and tender
towards you

Help me to love everyone, just as you do

My Rock

Laughter is in my soul, merriment in my spirit

Whatever the season, I'll praise God in it

I've founded my worth, my life on his rock

a foundation that cannot be shaken

No matter how the enemy fights, it cannot be taken

God's promises for our lives are as good as gold

That's why my trust in him will never grow old

He has set me upon a high boulder amongst the seas
and the flood

forgiven my iniquity and covered me in his blood

What rises against me cannot stand,

for I am placed in the palm of God's hand

His love brings laughter to my soul, merriment to
my spirit

God never fails, he put me in it to win it

My Source, My Shield

My source, my shield to you only I yield

Your voice speaks softly, like music to my ears

I love that you are concerned for me, guarding me
everyday

Holding me tight in your arms, never walking away

Though the enemy roars desiring to keep us apart

You live within me close to my heart

Your angels surrounding us my source, my shield

Everything I ask, you reveal

You have no replacement, some may come close

But it's of the Holy Spirit I will always boast

The gratitude that I speak is never enough

Thank you for the privilege of your tender touch

My Trust

My hope and reliance is in the Lord, who knows the
intimate secrets of my heart

I confide in him daily, pain and confusion he
thwarts

He keeps my mind in perfect peace, he keeps me
rooted as a strong tree

My total reliance is on the Lord, who speaks life to
me continually,

pushing me through the haze into everything that is
in store

I weep no more

He has placed his hand firmly on my shoulders,
whispering in my ear

More Like You

The closer that I get, the more that I desire to be like you

My steps ordered by benevolence and love

Wise as a serpent, yet harmless as a dove

Merciful and holy, proclaiming the cross boldly

Seeing the Christ in my neighbor, rebuking satan in the name of the Savior

The closer I get, the more that I desire to be like you

Forbearing all that displeases the Father

Believing God to part the water and allow me to cross on dry land

Tolerating whatever test at hand

Pressing forward towards the mark, though my tunnel may be dark,

You radiate at the end, my patience does not wear thin

I am blessed to be a servant to the ultimate friend,

who has been there from the beginning

Molding and making me built to win

More to God

There is more to God than judgment

More to God than rules

There's more to God than suffering

He has a plan for you

Free yourself from what you thought,

you will soon see

He is the answer for peace, joy, love, and all

provision

He gives liberally

Receive liberally

Give back even more, liberally

Most Treasured Gift

Father, you are a gift, the most treasured of all

You pulled me out of darkness when I answered
your call

I pray that you utilize me to bring deliverance to all

By your stripes we are healed, no condition too
small

Your aura is priceless, you make the weak stand tall

Your word speaks life abundantly

Each soul that reaches out to you, new life is
conceived

Your mysteries are revealed, hidden truths are
found

Father, you are a treasured gift that keeps giving,
may your grace continue to abound

New Beginning

Every day is a new beginning

When you awake from your sleep, a new chance is given

Put away the old and become new

Better than the day before

thinking wiser and expecting more

Reaching greater heights each day

My stumbling blocks are my stepping stones

Through my trials, I have grown

to be more acceptable in his sight

Girded with strength, full of might

Never Alone

Gracious is our God of many chances

He never walks away when we need him most

He holds us in his arms when we are tried and torn

dedicated to our forgiveness, slow to scorn

Alpha and Omega, ruler of all things

devoted to our salvation and making us clean

My adoration is ever for him

God never left my side when the road was dim

His love for me is like no other

greater than that of any father or mother

Run to him in you time of need

He will loose all shackles and make you free

Our Help

From the mountains and hills flow milk and
nourishment to the valley of our souls

Your power overtakes us in times of distress

You cause us to rise above all things and call us
blessed

With your spirit, we soar like an eagle with wings
stretched wide

From our battles, we no longer hide

God is with us to fight

As we turn our backs to darkness and walk into his
light

Behold the beauty of his presence and the warmth
of his essence

From the mountains and hills comes our help,

the Lord strong and mighty,

greater than ourselves

Our Keeper

You've kept our lives from destruction, protected us from mistakes

Even when out of your will we functioned, we still had your grace

Grateful to still be standing, no matter what the case

Positively knowing that I will see you face to face

Thank you for victory and triumphs over struggles everyday

You are our keeper when we try to walk away

I am happy to be a servant, without you I would be lost

I aim to stand by you at every cost

Nothing can repay all that you provide

My gratitude is to follow you, to rest and abide

Over Here!

My heart waits for you

To all of my mysteries, the key is in your hand

My eyes wait to see you move

My ears wait to hear you speak

My hope is to move in syncopation with you

That's why I live, that's why I breathe

Dear Father, use me

Peaceful

Peace among us you bring

Calmness like a stream

Fill us up like a river

Lover of our soul and heavy heart lifter

The magnificence of you splendor, will cause every
mind to surrender

Offering thanks to you this day

Your serenity will be present on earth as it in
heaven

Even when the storms raged and the earth shook

You brought stillness to our heart and flowed steady
as a brook

This day if we rely on you

we are guaranteed to victoriously make it through

You speak peace and tranquility to our hearts

While the world as we know it is falling apart

Your love prevails, you never change

We can depend on you in this latter rain

Pleasing My King

To do what is right in your eyes is filling my spirit
with life
My favor comes from pleasing you, my king,
creator of all things
All power belongs to you
How can I seek to only please man when the power
of death and life are in your hands?
By doing so, I would be building a house on sand
I am grateful for your willingness to bless me
For life long happiness, you are the key

Praise

I enter your gates with thanksgiving, your courts with praise

There is no place that I would rather be than blessing your holy name

Mountains, valleys, nor hell on earth can frustrate

Through it all, I will lay prostrate

My thrill is in worship, I can't get enough

You lift every burden, smooth all areas that are rough

Those who are truly submitted, no foul thing can remain

All must go and allow your spirit to reign

My focus is on my savior in whom I trust

The judge, jury, and executor, when all is said and done

So I continue to enter your gates with thanksgiving,

your courts with praise

There is no place I would rather be, than blessing your holy name

I magnify your name O God

There is nothing that I can say to compensate you for your grace and blessings that you have bestowed upon me

As high as the heavens, my praises can mount

The stature of them would still not amount to your everlasting fount of excellency, majesty, mercy given to me

if I could continuously say thank you every day, my words would never be an appropriate exaltation of your name

The tenderness that you have towards your children, who are diverse as you, is beyond measure

I count it an honor to be called one of yours, child of God the Holy Father

Pray-Through

I go to the Lord in prayer for all that I need

In the name of Jesus Christ, who feels my
infirmities

I pray that my children grow to be more faithful
than I

For wisdom, understanding, love, and might

Prayer is key, a lifeline, a source

Tap into it while in peace and at war

God loves to hear your voice, however, he gives us
a choice

Draw close to him and he will to you

Take the easy way out and pray your way through

Power of the Cross

Your power can never be undermined

The power of the cross has endured the test of time

Those who are feeble in their body, spirit, or mind

The power of the cross causes them to be capable
and secure, never to be left behind

By the power of the cross our enemies fail

You endow us with your might, allow us to stand
tall, be your light and prevail

Press Forward

The hour is far spent, time waits for no man

Will you surrender to him, or go by your own plans?

Infinite wisdom is available to those who seek

It requires confidence in he who reigns above all

Fear is not an option, it will only hold you back

Keeping you from promises, suffering from lack

Press forward no matter what,

into divine favor, never sheer luck

Purify

Your love sees though all of the muck and mire

Right through our brokenness, to what our soul
requires

Once you visit our heart we are never left the same

All things must go that defile your name

You speak to our hearts and they speak back to you

Lifting every burden, making them shiny and new

Purify and strengthen us as we call on your name

Our voices like a melody rise up,

bringing peace beyond understanding

Read, Pray, Listen

God speaks in many ways

When we refuse to listen, there is a lot to pay

Humble your heart, open your ears

His still voice will lead you and dry your tears

It will take you to your destiny

The road can be cluttered with many things

If you lose sight, you lose ground

You may get lost or turned around

He beckons, he calls

By our name, he knows us all

Remain focused on what's ahead

Read, pray, and listen, that is key

You will get to the place that you need to be

Reflections

When you look in the mirror, what do you see?

Is it a person striving to be what God has called you
to be?

Do you seek him first, or do your own thing?

Are you building a life in the image of the king?

His image is perfect, through God's guidance we
can also be

It is time to evaluate, listen to the instructions left
behind

Seek and you will find

a greater purpose and gifts from the divine-

to create a better you, built by design

For the master's use and the betterment of mankind

I ask you again, who do you see?

A reflection of you or a reflection of the king?

Reward

To be self -serving is a waste of time

Giving unto others with the heart of God is the key
to life

Great is the reward of those who hunger and thirst
for what is right

With hearts of compassion, love, and light

You give others wellness and strength to fight

Great is the reward of those who sow peace

In the middle of destruction and despair, the father
is pleased

Live each day not for what you can do for yourself

It's what you strive to do for others that brings you
happiness and true wealth

Sensitive to God

I am sensitive to your commands, I follow your
lead,

down the path of righteousness to fulfill my destiny

I hearken to your call, to whatever direction it may
lead

Knowing that you will supply my every need

You are the only one found to be constant and true-

your word never changing, I can always depend on
you

You are for me completely, genuinely, and tenderly

I do not become anxious, through it all, you defend
me

As long as I remain sensitive to your command, I
will move forward into your promised land

Sing Praises

From the bottom of my heart, I sing praises to my
Savior and King

The one who lifts me when I am down

Smooths my frown

Loosens my feet from the mire

Inside of my soul, he keeps a fire

I will not go a day without singing your praise,

for delivering me from being sin's slave

Speak to Me

Speak to my mind, sing to my heart

Your melodies and words satisfy my soul

They revive the old, breathe life into a corpse

Rain joy onto those who slumber and refuse to hear
your voice

Your emanation is like no other, it overtakes and
frees what is bound

As I seek you, life is found

Casting away old and replacing with new

Abundant and everlasting, all things referring to you

Your words speak to my heart and sing to my mind

Enabling me to bear the test of time

Stand Still

I will stand still and see the salvation of the Lord

God of forgiveness, mercy, and hope

He's right there at the end of the rope

He'll carry you through and keep your from defeat

A constant source of strength when you become
weak

He's the creator of time, so he is never late

Being careful not to stumble, on him I wait

I will keep my eyes on the prize until my dreams are
realized

I will stand still and see the salvation of the Lord,
this day!

Supernatural

His super with my natural enables me to win

I can conquer all with Christ, by day and night

I can overcome knowing that I was chosen by him
to fight,

From my mother's womb before I ever saw light

All that I encountered, composed my power,

causes me to stand and not be devoured

Not I alone, but he within

With his super and my natural, I will secure any
battle

Thankful

I am thankful for all of my prayers that you have answered,

allowing me to lie down in green pastures

Gifting me with love

Your light shining from above, brightening dark faces

Enabling me to walk in heavenly places

I am grateful for where you have brought me thus far

Believing for more, praising you for what is in store

Your excellence above all permits us to stand tall and bow low before you

Never ceasing to pray, bringing our worries to you for deliverance

Peace be still

The Diligent

Blessed are those who strive to please the Lord

He takes pleasure in our efforts, great is our reward

Those who see a need and will work to fulfill,

Will cause their own lives and another's to heal

He multiplies our harvest, supplies every need

brings gladness to our hearts and allows us to succeed

The peace in your mind is worth more than anything

Don't be weary in well-doing, your work is acknowledged-

if not by man, by the ruler of the land

The Door

The everlasting door, so grand, broad, and tall

Yet many never notice or go into it at all

God is summoning you to come into the gate

Don't walk away, wander, or go astray

The invitation has no expiration, go in without hesitation

It will ease your frustration

There is no command, only a call

Allow Him to be with you through it all

The Great Physician

Joy like a river you give to me

Your word heals so wonderfully

For the peace you bring, all praises are due

King of kings, I will forever trust you

Though your word is bound, it still never ends

New revelations you reveal again and again

To touch our hearts and mend our wounds

The Great Physician, let them who hurt come to you

The Harvest

Some ask when the harvest will be

Not realizing that every day we sow naturally

Good and bad, right and wrong

Some harvests come quickly, some take awfully

long

When it finally comes in, what will your harvest be?

Have you sown peace or insanity?

Will it be minute or will it yield great?

It's up to you to determine your fate

Think long and hard about the seeds that you sow

Whatever you plant is destined to grow

The Holy Spirit

His presence is here, I feel it within

Taking over my body like a rushing mighty wind

My thoughts are yielded, my hands lifted high

I gave my troubles to him and he became nigh

My body trembles as he takes over my tongue

Breaking every curse of destruction in the name of his Son

My heaviness is lifted, my mind is free

If you draw nigh to him, he will draw nigh to thee

The Long Road

There is a blessing in traveling the long road

Failing to comprehend,

I asked myself, "will this path ever end?"

Each little step brings me closer and stronger
everyday

As I look back and see what I've learned and what
I've gained

The sum is greater than what I've lost along the way

The road was not always lit, sometimes the scenery
was full of grit

I could have taken a bus, plane, or train

Because I didn't, a lot of folks thought I was insane

I chose to do it God's way, his hand is always near

Pushing me forward, encouraging me not to fear

You see, there's a blessing in taking the long road

Even though tests and trials litter the way

I know that my destination is only a prayer and a

step away

The Partaker's Eyes

Art is passion, art is life

It tells a story cheerful or solemn, vivid or dim

Well thought out, or result of a whim

Art's beauty is diverse

What is the norm? Acceptable or unacceptable?

It is admired, yet no one touches

Whether spoken, written, or painted with brushes

Each person has his or her own interpretation

All are different from what was in mind at the time
of creation

However, that's the excitement, the purpose

Freedom of thought and expression

The art of suggestion allows the imagination to
flow, minds to grow

Art begins conversations that would not ordinarily occur

One piece can put each person in a different world based on a story of their own lives

The meaning lies in the partaker's eyes

The Path Less Taken

I look to the hills and walk in victory

Looking forward beyond what my eyes can see

The path less taken is the one that is full of surprises

Stretching your mind and expanding your horizons

Pray for peace, as plentiful as the deep blue sea,

and the courage to travel everywhere that you need
to be

Freedom comes from being willing to make
mistakes

When you follow your heart, you realize it's less
that you make

The Power of the Cross

Your power can never be undermined

The power of the cross has endured the test of time

Those who are feeble in their body, spirit, or mind

The power of the cross causes them to be capable
and secure, never to be left behind

By the power of the cross our enemies fail

You endow us with your might, allow us to stand
tall, be your light and prevail

The Promise

What God has spoken to you will come to pass

I curse every force that speaks against his plan

Put the enemy in a choke hold and praise God now

It is not by chance that you were lost and found

God's promises are great, no man can override

Speak goodness and life, from his plan you cannot
hide

The treasures of God are waiting

Alpha and Omega has the final word

His thoughts are not our own

What He has spoken is already so, the enemy's
voice will not be heard

The Protector

Thank you for being my protection from every
harmful thing

From every danger seen and unseen

You go before me and make the crooked way
straight

Wise are those who hear your voice and do not stray

You are our strong tower and shield

In the city and the field

Your thoughtfulness of us is so unreal

Thank you for being our protector

The Reason

He's the reason I'm alive, the reason why I sing

The reason I never give up

The reason I still love, and why I'm secure

The reason that my future is so bright, why I have joy instead of sorrow

The reason that my children have a better tomorrow

The reason that I share hope with those that are in pain

The reason that I'm happy, even if there is no gain

His love is so great, so immeasurable

So good, delightful, and graceful

Incomparable

My God, full of grace, is the reason

The Right Fight

Life has struggle, struggle is a part of life

It's easy to get distracted from staying in the right
fight

Without focus cares will lead you astray

Make a commitment to renew yourself from day to
day

Seek bliss, delightment, and cheer

Always knowing that the one who loves you is near

Have a smile on your face, a melody in your heart

Refuse to let anger tear your life apart

Stay on the narrow path, without looking back

Resist being sidetracked by abundance or lack

You will arrive where you need to be

Trust and faithfulness is the key

Don't allow your emotions to take you into flight

Causing you to forget to stay in the right fight

The Sheep

A sheep I will always be to you

I allow you Lord to use me for what you need to do

I remain yielded to your call

A humble lamb, not a predator who scatters all

Continue to let your anointing reign

So that through me, people will never be the same

The Watcher

My heart belongs to you, the one who is tried and
true

You've been there all along, one relationship that
never goes wrong

I love you with all of my mind and soul, give me
peace until I grow old

My every thought will be of you

The one who loves me in spite of me, sees through
all of my tendencies

The watcher and giver of my needs

My heart I will continue to give unto thee

Tried and true, all good things come from you

Think Positively

Wonderful things start in the mind

Leave all negativity behind

Fill your thoughts with love, even take a walk in the park

Don't dwell on the bad things and allow your mind to grow dark

Wonderful, positive things start in the mind

Guard your thoughts and your heart, they are one of a kind :-)

Today

Gratefulness I am compelled to give

Those who believe in the Lamb, truly live

Take no thought for tomorrow, today is kind

You will always provide and give us new wine

In awe and amazement each day, your love renews
and shows us the way

Peace be still, what was crooked is now straight

You bring health to our body as we progress toward
our fate

Thank you for this new day, a new chance that you
keep giving

Incentive enough to me for righteous living

True and Living God

True and living God, Master and Savior on whom
we call

Who wipes our tears and picks us up when we fall

Your devotion allows us to stand through it all

We receive gifts from God, divine presents from the
Father

Miraculous healings that are long overdue, break
through today, we are depending on you

Deliverance and freedom to the spiritually bound,
every evil work will be cast down

Joy and peace to those in despair, lift up their
spirits, we know that you care

Overflow of blessings in places of lack, what has
been stolen, right now we take back

You are the true and living God

So grateful that you pour your Spirit over all

Help us to surrender to you until your final call

Trust and Obey

Bless the Lord with all of your heart

From his ways, do not depart

He will give you prosperity and peace

Reveal all that is hidden beneath

To love him is the best feeling of all

Obey and trust, He will never let you fall

Within his wings, you will abide

All that is evil will run and hide

I have joy and power to no end,

because of the father that lives within

From his love do not depart

He will give you the desires of your heart

Unmovable

Like a tree planted near the banks

Have unmovable, unshakable faith

Trouble may arise, opposition may how

Your belief will keep you if you don't back down

Keep your roots deeply and firmly planted in fertile
ground

Become stronger each year that comes around

For it is not by our own wisdom or might,

but He who sits high and looks down

Use Me

My gift to you is to be all that I can

to surrender everything that I am into your hands

You know me, you created me

with capabilities that only you understand

I bow in your presence, your virtue is so great

No matter how difficult the work is, I desire more

on my plate

I trust you, Lord, to lead me and guide me

into a wonderfully predicted fate

Victory

From the crown of our heads to the soles of our feet

Our God covers us and keeps us from defeat

When the tide is against us, you are always with us

Turning tables in our favor, allowing the glorious

to rise

Those who trust you and were despised,

have victory in the tough times

Proclaiming joy and hope, what matters most

We win in the end and live to tell the story of our

dear friend

War

You may encounter trouble that you did not ask for

The enemy may seek you out for war

You alone stand with an army

Surrounded by angels, no one can harm me

Keep your eyes on the prize and trust God above

Wear the whole armor and walk in love

Serenity shall surround you in times of turmoil

You are called blessed, your head anointed with oil

Stay in the battle, don't give up the fight

Be courageous, don't worry, darkness is always
overcome by the light

What Makes Sense

What makes sense to me is not always right,

My own feelings, I constantly fight

To be like Christ, I must be like a child

Willing to listen and follow in spite of,

what my own mind tells me to do

His capacity is greater than mine,

so I have to follow through recognizing that,

my faith in the father will not fail

Fear will only leave me in jail

What the father wants for me is liberty

Trust and believe

What makes sense to us is not always right

For the promises of God, we must relentlessly fight

Within

The search for happiness ends with you

All that we need is within ourselves

Discover what has been lost

Recover what was forgotten

Give thanks for what you have

Walk in peace towards what is to come

We are carriers of our own potential

Dreamers of our own dreams

Seers of our own visions

Leaders of our own destiny

All that we need is within ourselves

There isn't a need to look further

You are the miracle

Who's Calling?

Who's calling your name? It's me

Standing in need of your direction and protection

Open your arms to me, keep me in a place of refuge

Who's calling your name? It's me

I humbly bow before you, hungry for your presence

The glory of your essence fills me with cheer

With you right here, I decline to fear

Who's calling your name? It's me

Open the door to my future that I have been
preparing for

The one that you have shown time and time before

In my time of reflection I call on you, in Spirit and
in truth

Vapor

My life is but a vapor, after that is eternity

The way that I live determines where I will forever be

I choose to walk before you, let your light shine on my face

Listen to your soft whispers, follow your commands with haste

Let your love surround me, comfort me with grace

Allow your presence within me

Fill me with your sovereignty

Let your vision take over to see the unseen

My mouth speaks your words, filling the air with life

I will fulfill your purpose

There is no greater prize, than for my vapor to please you

This gift that we call life

Victory

From the crown of our heads to the soles of our feet

Our God covers us and keeps us from defeat

When the tide is against us, you are always with us

Turning tables in our favor, allowing the glorious

to rise

Those who trust you and were despised,

have victory in the tough times

Proclaiming joy and hope, what matters most

We win in the end and live to tell the story of our

dear friend

Your Love

Your love is never ending

Your tenderness and forgiveness flow like a river

That never dries, never stops

There is nothing that compares to the perfection of
your love

You are THE heaven sent, God above

Tranquility and peace flow from my heart

Breathtakingly beautiful melodies overtake my soul

You are wonderful, not one can take your place

This is my symbol of love for your amazing grace

Your True Friend

God is a true friend that never leaves your side

When trouble arises, he does not hide

He is right there no matter what the change

There is comfort when you do the same

There are life time benefits from being his true
friend

For keeping your trust when the light is dim

Remember to daily communicate

He will speak to you regarding your fate

God, indeed is a true friend who cares about you to
no end

Epilogue

He's so sweet, so lovely

Compassionate, considerate

Comforting

Always there when I call

He keeps all of his promises

His touch is like fire

His voice so soothing

He knows all about me, yet loves me

unconditionally

We will never leave each other

I'm the apple of his eye

JESUS

www.ingramcontent.com/pod-product-compliance
Lightning Source LLC
Chambersburg PA
CBHW021154020426
42331CB00003B/49